THE
TREASURE
OF
FRIENDSHIP

THE TREASURE OF
FRIENDSHIP

*Favorite Writings
About Enjoying
And Keeping Friends*

HALLMARK EDITIONS

The publisher wishes to thank those who have given their kind permission to reprint material included in this book. Every effort has been made to give proper acknowledgments. Any omissions or errors are deeply regretted, and the publisher, upon notification, will be pleased to make necessary corrections in subsequent editions.

ACKNOWLEDGMENTS:

Excerpt from *The Open Door* by Helen Keller. Copyright © 1957 by Helen Keller. Reprinted by permission of the publisher, Doubleday & Company, Inc. "Thank You, Friend" from *Poems of Inspiration and Courage* by Grace Noll Crowell. Copyright 1946 by Harper & Row, Publishers, Inc. Reprinted by permission of the publisher. Specified excerpt from page 344 of *Mark Twain's Notebook*, edited by Albert Bigelow Paine. Copyright 1935 by The Mark Twain Company. Reprinted by permission of Harper & Row Publishers, Inc. "Treasured Memories" from *Wind, Sand, and Stars* by Antoine de Saint-Exupéry, translated by Lewis Galantiere. Copyright 1939 by Antoine de Saint-Exupéry. Reprinted by permission of the publishers, Harcourt Brace Jovanovich, Inc. and William Heinemann Ltd. "Congeniality" from *The Pleasure of Your Company* by Frances Lester Warner. Copyright 1940 and 1968 by Frances Warner Hersey. Reprinted by permission of the publisher, Houghton Mifflin Company. "Truthfulness" from *The Business of Being a Friend* by Bertha Condé. Copyright 1916 by Bertha Condé. Reprinted by permission of the publisher, Houghton Mifflin Company. "Friendship's Growth" from *Essays* by Christopher Morley. Copyright 1927, renewed © 1955 by Christopher Morley. Reprinted by permission of J.B. Lippincott Company and the Estate of Christopher Morley. "A Friend Listens" from *A Child of the Century* by Ben Hecht. Copyright 1954. "The Primary Joy" from *Peace of Mind* by Joshua Loth Liebman. Copyright 1946 by Joshua Loth Liebman. "To Be a Friend" by Robert Hardy Andrews from *The Third Book of Words to Live By* edited by William Nichols. Copyright 1962. "Friendship Mending" by Frank Morley from *A New Treasury of Words to Live By* edited by William Nichols. Copyright 1959. All reprinted by permission of the publisher, Simon & Schuster, Inc.

WHAT a thing friendship is —
World without end!

ROBERT BROWNING

To Be a Friend

IN India 2500 years ago, a man named Gautama Buddha walked the roads and preached and taught. His teachings are still remembered by five hundred million Buddhist believers in Asia and the Orient.

I am not a Buddhist. But I find no disloyalty to my faith in accepting advice as practical today as it was when Buddha first offered it. In a mango grove in Bihar he told one of his disciples that five things are necessary to achieve release from unhappiness and fear. These, he said, include: restraint, proper discourse, energy in producing good thoughts, firmness in pursuing them, and acquisition of true insight. But first of all, and above all, he said, the seeker must learn to be a good friend.

5

When people asked for a definition of friendliness, Buddha answered, "It means to have hope of the welfare of others more than for one's self....It means affection unsullied by hope or thought of any reward on earth or in heaven."

Buddha admitted that such generous wholeheartedness would not be easy. Yet in the long run it is intensely practical. "Compassion and knowledge and virtue," he said, "are the only possessions that do not fade away."

"To be a good friend..." How simple it sounds — just five short words. Yet how much they represent! Think how much it could mean, a flowing out of new forces of friendship from person to person, and eventually from land to land.

Try as we may, there is no other form of security. As Buddha said, "Friendship is the only cure for

hatred, the only guarantee of
peace."

ROBERT HARDY ANDREWS

Congeniality

THE pleasure of your company is a
many-sided affair. It includes the
pleasure of seeing you, the pleasure
of hearing you talk, the drama of
watching your actions, your likes and
dislikes and adventures; the pleasure
of hunting you up in your haunts,
and the delicate flattery we feel when
you hunt us up in ours. We mean all
this and more when we say that we
find you "congenial."

Congeniality, when once established between two kindred spirits or
in a group, is the most carefree of
human relationships. It is effortless,
like purring. It is a basic theme in
friendship....

FRANCES LESTER WARNER

THE only way to have a friend is to
be one.

RALPH WALDO EMERSON

FRIENDSHIP is the shadow of the
evening, which strengthens with the
setting sun of life.

LA FONTAINE

The Rarest Faith

FRIENDSHIP takes place between those who have an affinity for one another, and is a perfectly natural and inevitable result. No professions or advances will avail. Even speech, at first, necessarily has nothing to do with it; but it follows after silence, as the buds in the graft do not put forth into leaves till long after the graft has taken. It is a drama in which the parties have no part to act....

Friendship is never established as an understood relation. Do you demand that I be less your friend that you may know it? Yet what right have I to think that another cherishes so rare a sentiment for me? It is a miracle which requires constant proofs. It is an exercise of the finest imagination and the rarest faith. It

says by a silent but eloquent be-
havior: "I will be so related to thee as
thou canst not imagine; even so thou
mayest believe. I will spend truth, all
my wealth on thee," and the friend
responds silently through his nature,
and life, and treats his friend with the
same divine courtesy....

The language of Friendship is not
words but meaning. It is an in-
telligence above language. One imag-
ines endless conversations with his
friend, in which the tongue shall be
loosed, and thoughts be spoken,
without hesitancy, or end; but the
experience is commonly far otherwise....

Suppose you go to bid farewell to
your friend who is setting out on a
journey; what other outward sign do
you know than to shake his
hand?...There are some things which
a man never speaks of, which are
much finer kept silent about. To the

highest communications we only lend a silent ear....In human intercourse the tragedy begins, not when there is misunderstanding about words, but when silence is not understood.

HENRY DAVID THOREAU

THE holy passion of Friendship is so sweet and steady and loyal and enduring a nature that it will last through a whole lifetime, if not asked to lend money.

MARK TWAIN

A New World

I awoke this morning with devout thanksgiving for my friends, the old and the new. Shall I not call God the Beautiful, who daily showeth himself so to me in his gifts. I chide society, I embrace solitude, and yet I am not so ungrateful as not to see the wise, the lovely and the noble-minded, as from time to time they pass my gate. Who hears me, who understands me, becomes mine — a possession for all time. Nor is Nature so poor but she gives me this joy several times, and thus we weave social threads of our own, a new web of relations; and, as many thoughts in succession substantiate themselves, we shall by and by stand in a new world of our own creation, and no longer strangers and pilgrims in a traditionary globe. My friends have to come to me unsought. The great God gave them to me.

RALPH WALDO EMERSON

Always a Friend

A true friend unbosoms freely, advises justly, assists readily, adventures boldly, takes all patiently, defends courageously, and continues a friend unchangeably. In short, choose a friend as thou dost a wife, till death separate you. Death cannot kill what never dies. Nor can spirits ever be divided that love and live in the same Divine Principle. This is the comfort of friends, that though they may be said to die, yet their friendship and society are, in the best sense, ever present, because immortal.

WILLIAM PENN

Understanding and Trust

THE very best thing is good talk, and the thing that helps it most is *friendship*. How it dissolves the barriers that divide us, and loosens all constraints, and diffuses itself like some fine old cordial through all the veins of life — this feeling that we understand and trust each other, and wish each other heartily well! Everything into which it really comes is good. It transforms letterwriting from a task to a pleasure. It makes music a thousand times more sweet. The people who play and sing not *at us*, but *to us* — how delightful it is to listen to them! Yes, there is a talk-ability that can express itself even without words. There is an exchange of thoughts and feelings which is happily alike in speech and in silence. It is quietness pervaded with friendship.

HENRY VAN DYKE

Not in Vain

IF I can stop one heart
from breaking,
I shall not live in vain;
If I can ease one life the aching,
Or cool one pain,
Or help one fainting robin
Unto his nest again,
I shall not live in vain.

EMILY DICKINSON

A Perfect Union

WHAT we commonly call friends and friendships are nothing but an acquaintance and connection, contacted either by accident or upon some design, by means of which there happens some little intercourse betwixt our souls. But, in the friendship I speak of, they mingle and melt into one piece, with so universal a mixture that there is left no more sign of the seam by which they were first conjoined. If any one should ask why I loved [a friend] I feel it could not otherwise be expressed than by making answer, "Because it was he; because it was I." There is, beyond what I am able to say, I know not what inexplicable and inevitable power that brought on this union.

MONTAIGNE

Thank You, Friend

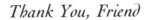 I never came to you, my friend,
And went away without
Some new enrichment of the heart:
More faith, and less of doubt,
More courage for the days ahead,
And often in great need
Coming to you, I went away
Comforted, indeed.

How can I find the shining words,
The glowing phrase that tells
All that your love has meant to me,
All that your friendship spells?
There is no word, no phrase for you
On whom I so depend.
All I can say to you is this:
God bless you, precious friend.

GRACE NOLL CROWELL

The Friend Who Just Stands By

WHEN trouble comes your soul
   to try,
You love the friend who just
   "stands by."
Perhaps there's nothing he can do —
The thing is strictly up to you;
For there are troubles all your own,
And paths the soul must tread alone;
Times when love cannot smooth the
   road
Nor friendship lift the heavy load,
But just to know you have a friend
Who will "stand by" until the end,
Whose sympathy through all endures,
Whose warm handclasp is always
   yours —
It helps, someway, to pull you through,
Although there's nothing he can do.
And so with fervent heart you cry,
"God bless the friend who just
   'stands by.'"

                              B. Y. WILLIAMS

A Friendship Toast

MAY you live
as long as you like,
and have all that you like
as long as you live.

ANONYMOUS

FRIENDSHIP improves happiness,
and abates misery, by doubling our
joy, and dividing our grief.

JOSEPH ADDISON

Accept My Full Heart's Thanks

YOUR words came just when needed.
  Like a breeze
Blowing and bringing from the
      wide soft sea
Some cooling spray, to meadow
      scorched with heat
    And choked with dust and clouds
      of sifted sand
That hateful whirlwinds, envious
      of its bloom,
Had tossed upon it. But the
    cool sea breeze
Came laden with the odors of the sea
    And damp with spray, that laid
      the dust and sand,
And brought new life and strength
      to blade and bloom,
    So words of thine came over
      miles to me,
    Fresh from the mighty sea, a
      true friend's heart,

And brought me hope, strength,
    and swept away
  The dusty webs that human
    spiders spun
Across my path. Friend — and
    the word means much —
  So few there are who reach
    like thee, a hand
Up over all the barking curs of spite
  And give the clasp, when most
    its need is felt,
Friend, newly found, accept my
    full heart's thanks.

ELLA WHEELER WILCOX

WHAT is friendship? One soul in two bodies.

ARISTOTLE

The Greatest Happiness

LIFE is to be fortified by many friendships. To love, and to be loved, is the greatest happiness. If I lived under the burning sun of the equator, it would be pleasure for me to think that there were many human beings on the other side of the world who regarded and respected me; I could not live if I were alone upon the earth, and cut off from the remembrance of my fellow-creatures. It is not that a man has occasion often to fall back upon the kindness of his friends; perhaps he may never experience the necessity of doing so; but we are governed by our imaginations, and they stand there as a solid and impregnable bulwark against all the evils of life.

SYDNEY SMITH

New Friends and Old Friends

MAKE new friends, but keep
the old;
Those are silver, these are gold.
New-made friendships, like new wine,
Age will mellow and refine.
Friendships that have stood the test —
Time and change — are surely best;
Brow may wrinkle, hair grow gray;
Friendship never knows decay.
For 'mid old friends, tried and true,
Once more we our youth renew.
But old friends, alas! may die;
New friends must their place supply.
Cherish friendship in your breast —
New is good, but old is best;
Make new friends, but keep the old;
Those are silver, these are gold.

JOSEPH PARRY

Old Friends

OLD friends are the great blessing of one's latter years. Half a word conveys one's meaning. They have a memory of the same events, and have the same mode of thinking. I have young relations that may grow upon me, for my nature is affectionate, but can they grow old friends?

HORACE WALPOLE

A Friend Listens

I have noted that the best and closest friends are those who seldom call on each other for help. In fact, such is almost the finest definition of a friend — a person who does not need us but who is able to enjoy us.

I have seldom suffered over the troubles of a friend. Are his mishaps short of tragedy, I am inclined to chuckle. And he is seldom serious in telling me of his misfortunes. He makes anecdotes out of them, postures comically in their midst and tries to entertain me with them. This is one of the chief values of my friendship, as it is of his. We enable each other to play the strong man superior to his fate. Given a friend to listen, my own disasters change color. I win victories while relating them. Not only have I a friend "on my side" who will believe my version of the battle — and permit me to seem a victor in my communiques — but I have actually a victory in me. I am able to show my friend my untouched side. My secret superiority to bad events becomes stronger when I can speak and have a friend believe in it.

BEN HECHT

The Warmth of Friendship

AS you say, we don't need soft skies to make friendship a joy to us. What a heavenly thing it is; "World without end," truly. I grow warm thinking of it, and should glow at the thought if all the glaciers of the Alps were heaped over me! Such friends God has given me in this little life of mine!

CELIA THAXTER

A slender acquaintance with the world must convince every man that actions, not words, are the true criterion of the attachment of friends; and that the most liberal professions of goodwill are very far from being the surest marks of it.

GEORGE WASHINGTON

Friend of a Wayward Hour

FRIEND of a wayward hour,
you came
Like some good ghost, and went
the same;
And I within the haunted place
Sit smiling on your vanished face
And talking with — your name.
But thrice the pressure of
your hand —
First hail — congratulations — and
Your last "God bless you!" as
the train
That brought you snatched you
back again
Into the unknown land.
"God bless me?" Why, your
very prayer
Was answered ere you asked it there,
I know — for when you came to lend
Me your kind hand, and call me friend,
God blessed me unaware.

JAMES WHITCOMB RILEY

To Our Guest

IF you come cheerily,
Here shall be jest for you.
If you come wearily,
Here shall be rest for you.
If you come borrowing,
Gladly we'll loan to you.
If you come sorrowing,
Love shall be shown to you.
Under our thatch, friend,
Place shall abide for you.
Touch but the latch, friend,
The door shall swing wide for you!

NANCY BYRD TURNER

The Habit of Friendship

AS widowers proverbially marry again, so a man with the habit of friendship always finds new friends....My old age judges more charitably and thinks better of mankind than my youth ever did. I discount idealization, I forgive one-sidedness, I see that it is essential to perfection of any kind. And in each person I catch the fleeting suggestion of something beautiful, and swear eternal friendship with that.

GEORGE SANTAYANA

Friendship's Growth

FRIENDSHIPS do not grow up in any carefully tended and contemplated fashion.... They begin haphazard.

As we look back on the first time we saw our friends we find that generally our original impression was curiously astray. We have worked along beside them, have consorted with them drunk or sober, have grown to cherish their delicious absurdities, have outrageously imposed on each other's patience — and suddenly we awoke to realize what had happened.

We had, without knowing it, gained a new friend. In some curious way the unseen border line had been passed. We had reached the final culmination of Anglo-Saxon regard when two men rarely look each other straight in the eyes because they are ashamed to show each other how fond they are.

We had reached the fine flower and the ultimate test of comradeship — that is, when you get a letter from one of your "best friends," you know you don't need to answer it until you get ready to.

CHRISTOPHER MORLEY

THE proper office of a friend is to side with you when you are in the wrong. Nearly anybody will side with you when you are in the right.

MARK TWAIN

Truthfulness

EVERY friendship that lasts is built of certain durable materials. The first of these is truthfulness. If I cannot look into the eyes of my friend and speak out always the truthful thought and feeling with the simplicity of a little child, there can be no real friendship between us. Friends who have to be "handled" or "managed," or with whom we take refuge in fencing or posing, do not know the love that casts out fear. "Trust is the first requisite for making a friend," says Hugh Black, "faithfulness is the first requisite for keeping him"; and trust and faithfulness cannot endure without truthfulness.

BERTHA CONDÉ

In Constant Repair

I have often thought that as longevity is generally desired, and I believe generally expected, it would be wise to be continually adding to the number of our friends, that the loss of some may be supplied by others.

Friendship, "the wine of life," should be like a well-stocked cellar, be thus continually renewed; and it is consolatory to think, that although we can seldom add what will equal the generous first-growth, yet friendship becomes insensibly old in much less time than is commonly imagined, and not many years are required to make it very mellow and pleasant.

Warmth will, no doubt, make considerable difference. Men of affectionate temper and bright fancy will coalesce a great deal sooner than those who are cold and dull.

This [proposition] was the opinion of [Dr. Samuel] Johnson himself. He said to Sir Joshua Reynolds, "If a man does not make new acquaintances through life, he will soon find himself left alone. A man, Sir, should keep his friendships in constant repair."

JAMES BOSWELL

Comfortably Together

MY coat and I live comfortably together.

It has assumed all my wrinkles, does not hurt me anywhere, has moulded itself on my deformities, and is complacent to all my movements, and I only feel its presence because it keeps me warm. Old coats and old friends are the same thing.

VICTOR HUGO

The Primary Joy

THE primary joy of life is acceptance, approval, the sense of appreciation and companionship of our human comrades. Many men do not understand that the need for fellowship is really as deep as the need for food, and so they go throughout life accepting many substitutes for genuine, warm, simple relatedness.

JOSHUA LOTH LIEBMAN

Tokens of Love

GET not your friends by bare compliments, but by giving them sensible tokens of your love. It is well worthwhile to learn how to win the heart of man the right way. Force is of no use to make or preserve a friend, who is an animal that is never caught and tamed but by kindness and pleasure. Excite them by your civilities, and show them that you desire nothing more than their satisfaction; oblige with all your soul that friend who has made you a present of his own.

SOCRATES

Friendship Mending

A man, Sir, should keep his friendships in constant repair.

SAMUEL JOHNSON

THESE words from Johnson entered into me as a boy and ever since then have quietly exerted a power of compulsion. I think it was the oddness of the wording which first startled me. Was friendship a thing to be repaired, as if with hammer and nails? Did Johnson mean you should consciously go around, as politicians do, mending fences? I thought I knew what friendship was, and that when it occurred it was just natural, not something to be carpentered.

Yet the simple and puzzling phrase stayed in my mind till suddenly one day the meaning came clear: You can't take friendship for granted. It always needs repair. Cross your two fingers — and even people as close as that can lose touch. They can drift apart. Friendship is something you can't buy and can't command, but you can lose. So it must be refreshed. At all times, and before too late, it needs refreshment.

How, then, does one go about refreshing friendship? "On clean-shirt day," wrote Johnson's biographer, "he went abroad, and paid visits." That was his way. But to my mind the specific details of repairing friendship are not very important. Sound friendships consist of many nameless acts. What matters is the intent — the intent to keep alive something worthy and mutual. This happens when people remember each other, cultivate each other, meet each other a little more than halfway. Such are the ways in which friendship may be shared.

Nothing on earth is more important, for, just as it has been said that
"to lose a friend is to die a little," so
the reverse is also true, and when you
keep a friend you add something to
the richness and the worth of life.

FRANK V. MORLEY

Woman as Friend

IT is a wonderful advantage to a man, in every pursuit or avocation, to secure an adviser in a sensible woman. In woman there is at once a subtle delicacy of tact, and a plain soundness of judgment, which are rarely combined to an equal degree in man.

A woman, if she be really your friend, will have a sensitive regard for your character, honor, repute. She will seldom counsel you to do a shabby thing; for a woman friend always desires to be proud of you. At the same time, her constitutional timidity makes her more cautious than your male friend. She, therefore, seldom counsels you to do an imprudent thing. By friendships, I mean pure friendships — those in which there is no admixture of the passion of love, except in the married state.

A man's best female friend is a wife of good sense and good heart, whom he loves, and who loves him. If he have that, he need not seek elsewhere. But suppose the man to be without such a helpmate, female friendship he must have, or his intellect will be without a garden, and there will be many an unheeded gap even in its strongest fence.

Better and safer, of course, are such friendships, where disparities of years or circumstances put the idea of love out of the question. Middle life has rarely this advantage: youth and age have. Moliere's old housekeeper was a great help to his genius; and Montaigne's philosophy takes both a gentler and loftier character of wisdom from the date in which he finds, in Marie de Gournay, an adopted daughter.

SIR EDWARD BULWER-LYTTON

Small Service

SMALL service is true service while it lasts;
  Of friends, however humble, scorn
    not one;
The daisy, by the shadow that it
  casts,
    Protects the lingering dewdrop
      from the sun.

WILLIAM WORDSWORTH

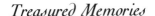

Treasured Memories

OLD friends cannot be created out of hand. Nothing can match the treasure of common memories, of trials endured together, of quarrels and reconciliations and generous emotions....We forget that there is no hope of joy except in human relations.

ANTOINE DE SAINT-EXUPÉRY

Good Conversation

THE mind never unbends itself so
agreeably as in the conversation of a
well-chosen friend. There is indeed
no blessing of life that is any way
comparable to the enjoyment of a
discreet and virtuous friend. It eases
and unloads the mind, clears and
improves the understanding, engen-
ders thought and knowledge, ani-
mates virtue and good resolutions,
soothes and allays the passions, and
finds employment for most of the
vacant hours of life.

JOSEPH ADDISON

LIFE is a chronicle of friendship. Friends create the world anew each day. Without their loving care, courage would not suffice to keep hearts strong for life.

HELEN KELLER

Set in Cochin, produced by
Fonderie G. Peignot & Fils
in 1913. Its hand-engraved
appearance blends harmoniously
with the 18th Century fleurons
from the Andrew Szoeke collection
used in this edition. Printed on
Hallmark Eggshell Book paper.
Designed by Terri Sheldon.